GW00374444

GIFT *of* GRACE

GIFT *of*
GRACE

Little Inspirations That Invite God's Blessings

Candy Chand

FAIR WINDS
PRESS
GLOUCESTER, MASSACHUSETTS

First published in the U.S.A. by
Fair Winds Press
33 Commercial Street
Gloucester, Massachusetts 01930-5089

Library of Congress Cataloging-in-Publication Data

Chand, Candy.
  Gift of grace : little inspirations that invite God's blessings /
Candy Chand.
     p.   cm.
   ISBN 1-931412-20-0
   1. Cardinal virtues. 2. Spiritual life—Christianity. I. Title.
BV4645.C47 2003
241'.4—dc21   2002153601

10 9 8 7 6 5 4 3 2 1

Cover design and illustration by Leeann Leftwich Zajas
Design by Leeann Leftwich Zajas

Printed and bound in Canada

To all who seek the blessing of divine grace

CONTENTS

ACKNOWLEDGMENTS

I'd like to offer a special thank-you
to the following people:

To Paula Munier—a wonderful editor whose
support of my work remains greatly appreciated, and to
Brenda Manginelli—for allowing me quiet office
moments to develop this manuscript.

INTRODUCTION

The sacred blessing of grace is not attainable through sheer determination. Grace, by definition, is the gift of unmerited favor. By understanding the role virtue plays in our lives and our relationships with others, we're able to abundantly reap the fruits of a loving, divine plan. The seven spiritual virtues—hope, charity, justice, temperance, prudence, fortitude, and faith—give us a hint of God's character. By unwrapping these sacred treasures and incorporating their divine essence into our being, we can give, as well as receive, unimaginable joy.

Through the pages of this book, it is my hope you'll be inspired to re-evaluate your purpose, your destiny, and your desires, so that you may incorporate the wealth of divine grace into your life. Take your time as you read the following passages.

Consider writing in your journal along the way, creating a sacred dialogue between your soul and your Creator. You'll soon discover new purpose, new direction, and new joy emerging from the foundation of your being. It's never too late to embrace fresh journeys, purpose, and inspired intent for your life. And it's never too late to place yourself in the path of God's divine grace

May this book open your heart toward new blessings—in your spirit and for those who cross your path. And may the gift of grace be yours.

HOPE

The miserable have no other medicine
but only hope.

WILLIAM SHAKESPEARE

Hope—the virtue of longing for what you hold dear, a desire deep within your heart, grasped tightly even against immeasurable odds. What makes an aspiring artist toil for years believing that someday the work will be rewarded? What makes anyone who's lost, shattered, and isolated hang on to the dream of soon finding someone to love? What makes parents trust, despite contrary scientific evidence, that their dying child will not only recover but also go on to live a healthy, productive, and happy life? It's hope: the God-given virtue cherished throughout the world.

But hope can be shattered. Discouragement, disappointment, and doubt can rage through our souls until even fragments of its light seem impossible to grasp. Yet within us lies the ability to reach out, to ask the Creator for the virtue of hope, inspiring us to continue our spiritual journey in peace. Yes, times of waiting can be difficult. God understands our human frustration, however, and he has offered great comfort in his Word. Scripture teaches us about the dark times, when we may wait hours, days, or even years for our dreams to come true.

Hope deferred maketh the heart sick:
but when the desire cometh, it is a tree of life.

PROVERBS 13:12

Have you been waiting so long that hope seems like a remote, lost memory? Have time and discouragement caused you to give up and surrender your dreams? Are you in a dark, shadowy place so deep it seems impossible to find your way out? Yes, loss of hope breeds anguish. Yet if even a spark remains in your heart, you'll retain the strength to go on.

Years ago, my friend Karen was going through difficult times. Her finances were a mess and her relationships even worse. She was a young girl, only 20, but so discouraged she lost all sense of hope. One day, as she drove down a long, winding road, she quietly whispered, "I wish I were dead." Within a split second, a large commercial truck came barreling out of nowhere and crossed the centerline, headed right for her car. Thank goodness Karen's reactions were swift. She managed to swerve just in time and landed in a ditch, narrowly escaping death. As she sat in her car shaking, she felt the awesome presence of God and a clear awareness of the error of her ways. By losing hope and concentrating on death, Karen had left herself open for destruction. She has learned her lesson well. Now she's thankful for what she has, difficulties and all, and maintains a positive way of viewing even troubling circumstances. Today Karen embraces the virtue of hope, a virtue that springs forth life instead of death. Countless individuals have experienced the intense destruction manifested by loss of hope. Another friend, Jamie, was unhappily married for years. However, when her husband made the decision to leave, Jamie was devastated, unwilling to admit defeat. Shortly afterward, in moments of her darkest hour, she discovered lumps in her neck. In a panic, she called her doctor for medical advice, and within days, she was diagnosed with terminal cancer. Surprisingly, Jamie felt strangely relieved after hearing the news. One chilly afternoon, as she sought God in prayer, she felt him speak deep within her soul. Jamie, it seemed, was so determined to stay married that she was willing to die rather than survive a divorce. Shocked by the stark realization, she asked God to forgive her, then to engulf her mind with new, positive thoughts. As her spirit lifted and the virtue of hope filled her existence, her cancer amazingly went into spontaneous remission, never to return again. Now by sharing these two stories, I'm not saying disease and death are caused by negative thoughts. It's simply not true. We live in a fallen world, and death and suffering are all around us. However, I'm convinced that these women were passively toying with suicide and therefore reaped devastating results, until their hope was finally restored.

Although at times we may feel abandoned by our Creator, such a premise couldn't be farther from the truth. According to Saint Augustine, God will never betray our hope.

God is not a deceiver, that he should offer to support us, and then, when we lean upon Him, should slip away from us.

SAINT AUGUSTINE

Tell me—where do you place your hope? Does it rest in yourself, in your own abilities, or in God's divine nature to seek out what's best for his children? Surely everyone has given talents and gifts that can bring to pass a multitude of dreams, but to fulfill the calling for which we were created, we must place our hope in the goodness of God. Even when we feel alone, scripture teaches us, God is always watching. He sees our needs and desires to meet them with loving compassion.

Be of good courage, and he shall strengthen your heart,
all ye that hope in the Lord.

PSALM 31:24

During times of great discouragement and weakness, it's human nature to hope in our own strength or the strength of those we lean on so desperately. In reality, there's nothing wrong with interdependence in this world—joyfully using our own talents, as well as those around us. However, for most of us, it's when all else fails that we begin to seek God and place our hope in him. These very disappointments and failures drive us to the one who's been waiting patiently all along with the answers, the one in whom our hope should rest in quiet confidence all along. What clever strategy he uses! The God of the Universe waits patiently as we stumble about, putting hope in every possible solution but his, only to rejoice when we come humbly before him seeking his help. George MacDonald deeply understood our need to hope in God as our ultimate source of help.

How often we look upon God as our last and feeblest resource! We go to Him because we have nowhere else to go. And then we learn that the storms of life have driven us, not upon the rocks, but into the desired haven.

GEORGE MACDONALD

Distractions, disappointments, and discouragement can limit our ability to cling to hope. Yet if you've been promised a gift by the Creator and if his still, small voice tells you your dream will come to pass, then hang on to hope, even when no one else seems to be giving you any.

Yes, years may go by before your dream is fulfilled. Sometimes the vision will be realized in ways you've never imagined. I once knew a gentleman whose mother was convinced he was called to the ministry.

As years went on and he had not executed the vision, she stubbornly held on to hope. Then one day, she discovered a new reality. Without any fanfare, her son had been diligently working in a halfway house for troubled teens, counseling them through difficult and treacherous times.

It was then that she realized her hope had been fulfilled. Her son was ministering to the world, just not in the way she'd ever expected. In scripture, we're told of people waiting, praying, and hoping endlessly for God's vision to come true.

Let's briefly examine Abraham's life. Abraham was a simple man whose heart embraced God. One day, the Lord promised Abraham a child—an offspring that would father great nations.

Yet Abraham was old, and so was his wife! In all reality, the Lord's promise seemed humanly impossible. Through it all (and you can bet despite laughter from his neighbors), Abraham continued to believe.

In fact, scripture shows he continued to hope for years. *Who against hope believed in hope, that he might become the father of many nations, according to that which was spoken, So shall thy seed be.*

And being not weak in faith, he considered not his own body now dead, when he was about a hundred years old, nor the deadness of Sarah's womb:

He staggered not at the promise of God through unbelief;

but was strong in faith, giving glory to God; And being fully persuaded

that, what he had promised, he was able also to perform. And

therefore it was imputed to him for righteousness.

ROMANS 4:18–22

And guess what? Abraham's dedication, faith, and commitment to the virtue of hope, even against all odds, were magnificently rewarded. In time, his son was born—a child of God's promise. Certainly life can be difficult. We often struggle about, searching for our way, yet we're promised that God will walk with us, even though the path may be dark and long. Whether we're alone or with loved ones, in life or in death, in joy or in sorrow, he is always there. Nothing displays this virtue better than the Twenty-third Psalm, offered as a light of hope to the world.

The Lord is my shepherd; I shall not want. He maketh me
to lie down in green pastures: he leadeth me beside the still waters.
He restoreth my soul: he leadeth me in the paths of righteousness for
his name's sake. Yea, though I walk through the valley of the shadow of
death, I will fear no evil: for thou art with me; thy rod and thy staff
they comfort me. Thou preparest a table before me in the presence of
mine enemies: thou anointest my head with oil; my cup runneth over.
Surely goodness and mercy shall follow me all the days of my
life: and I will dwell in the house of the Lord for ever.

PSALM 23

How long must we hold on to hope? Is there a time limit when it's safe to move on, get a new dream, and cast our former promises to the wind? To best answer that question, meditate once again on Abraham, who discovered that some things just don't happen overnight. As he did, we should place our hope in God. He will work it out, in his time and for our own good. Despite our demands, his calendar isn't marked off with our quick "to do" list. He's simply not in a hurry, because in the eternal scheme of things, time is irrelevant. Scripture reveals a different timetable than most of us impatient humans can comprehend.

But, beloved, be not ignorant of this one thing, that one day is with the Lord as a thousand years, and a thousand years as one day.

---

2 PETER 3:8

In order to rest in hope, it's vital we draw close to the Creator. Without intimate contact, time spent in prayer, our candle of hope will become dim or go out altogether. For in this tight-knit relationship, we become aware that we can count on God's miraculous intervention during times of difficulty or even attack. The psalmist David, although often discouraged, deeply understood that to embrace hope, we must rest in the arms of the one who grants us such virtue.

He that dwelleth in the secret place of the most High shall abide under the shadow of the Almighty. I will say of the LORD, He is my refuge and my fortress: my God; in him will I trust. Surely he shall deliver thee from the snare of the fowler, and from the noisome pestilence. He shall cover thee with his feathers, and under his wings shalt thou trust: his truth shall be thy shield and buckler. Thou shalt not be afraid for the terror by night; nor for the arrow that flieth by day; nor for the pestilence that walketh in darkness; nor for the destruction that wasteth at noonday. A thousand shall fall at thy side, and ten thousand at thy right hand; but it shall not come nigh thee. Only with thine eyes shalt thou behold and see the reward of the wicked. Because thou hast made the LORD, which is my refuge, even the most High, thy habitation; There shall no evil befall thee, neither shall any plague come nigh thy dwelling. For he shall give his angels charge over thee, to keep thee in all thy ways. They shall bear thee up in their hands, lest thou dash thy foot against a stone. Thou shalt tread upon the lion and adder: the young lion and the dragon shalt thou trample under feet. Because he hath set his love upon me, therefore will I deliver him: I will set him on high, because he hath known my name. He shall call upon me, and I will answer him: I will be with him in trouble; I will deliver him, and honour him. With long life will I satisfy him, and show him my salvation.

PSALM 91:1–4

Yes, we can count on our Creator to help us in times of need. We can hope even when life's problems seem overwhelming. Rest assured, God never sleeps on the job. When we're in need, our hope must lie in his strength, in his love, and in his desire to see us through.

Despite our optimistic plans, circumstances can be daunting. Several years ago, while going through a horrific legal dispute, I found myself slipping into hopelessness. After a monumental betrayal, I had great difficulty struggling with the fragments of ultimate injustice. I prayed constantly for a fair solution, but after several years of trouble, I resigned myself to despair. One afternoon, when I could no longer bear the pain any longer, I sank to the ground, begging God to restore the virtue of hope.

I felt as if I'd been hanging on to the side of a mountain for years, and I simply couldn't hold on any longer. Without a doubt, my sanity was slipping away. I was about to let go, plummeting hopelessly to the emotional bottom.

In my anguished state, I didn't ask God to bring me to the top of that mountain because at that point, I couldn't imagine such wonderful restoration. I simply asked him to grab my hand and hold on to me, so I could safely let go.

From that moment on, the hopelessness, panic, and dark reality lifted. I was in God's hands. My hope rested firmly in him.

Throughout scripture, we see others struggling through great difficulties; even King David suffered from the dark valleys of hopelessness. Yet for thousands of years, the Psalm scriptures have soothed many weary souls. David knew our hope must rest not in our armies, our career, our kingdom, or our riches but in the One who holds everything in his hands.

I will lift up mine eyes unto the hills, from

whence cometh my help. My help cometh from the Lord,

which made heaven and earth. He will not suffer thy foot

to be moved: he that keepeth thee will not slumber. Behold, he that

keepeth Israel shall neither slumber nor sleep. The Lord is thy keeper:

the Lord is thy shade upon thy righthand. The sun shall not smite thee

by day, nor the moon by night. The Lord shall preserve thee from all

evil: he shall preserve thy soul. The Lord shall preserve thy going

out and thy coming in from this time forth,

and even for evermore.

PSALM 121

In times of trouble or discouragement, cling to the Psalms. Ask God to restore good, positive thoughts into your life, lighting up your path and indwelling your spirit with divine hope.

Tips for Embracing
the Virtue of Hope

* Read scripture, especially the Psalms. God's promises will inspire faith in his goodness in times of trouble.

* When trapped in despair, ask the Creator for the gift of hope to restore your spirit.

* Spend time in prayer. For in this intimate relationship, we can grasp God's love and power to help us in our time of need

* Dwell on the positive. If your hope is fleeting and you dwell on negative thoughts, you're sure to attract more trouble your way.

* Don't expect your dreams to turn out exactly as you've planned or according to your schedule. Remember, God's timing is perfect, and his plan for your life is far better than you can imagine.

CHARITY

We are all pencils in the hand of a writing God,
who is sending love letters to the world.

MOTHER TERESA OF CALCUTTA

Charity—the virtue of love, kindness, and a spirit of benevolence toward others. How easy it is to care for those we naturally gravitate to, those who have similar goals and lifestyles, and those who are close at hand, present right before our eyes. To reach out beyond those limitations to a place far greater, one that envelops all of God's creations as worthy of love, is a far higher calling. Mother Teresa, adored worldwide for her infinite acts of compassion, taught us much about charity in its highest form, simply because she chose to love those who weren't highly esteemed by others—the sick, the destitute, and the hopeless.

And she did this at great, personal sacrifice, leaving behind the riches of this world in pursuit of pleasing her God. Because of her commitment to the virtue of charity, countless lives were changed as she reached out in love, calling upon a higher power than her own to touch the hearts of humanity.

Many of us will never travel farther than our own backyards. Yet we can still bless others—our family, our coworkers, our neighbors—and even our own spirits by offering gestures of kindness as we soothe the aches of a hurting world, bruised by troubles on every side.

We're implored to give our hearts in love—to reach out to others in acts of genuine compassion. The power of charity, the gift of love, is honored in scripture as a holy virtue.

...giving all diligence, add to your faith virtue; and to virtue knowledge; and to knowledge temperance; and to temperance patience; and to patience godliness; and to godliness brotherly kindness; and to brotherly kindness charity.

---

2 PETER 1:5–7

But how can you make a difference? Perhaps you will not travel halfway around the world to soothe a troubled soul. Instead, offering a simple word of encouragement will be your gift to someone desperately in need. As people all around you cry out for help, even if in small whispers of quiet grief, be compelled to offer them the hope that dwells within you. It may not seem a dramatic rescue, yet a simple act of kindness may mean as much to your suffering neighbor as a lifeline to a drowning soul.

During her 1979 Nobel Peace Prize acceptance speech in Oslo, Norway, Mother Teresa spoke of a Hindu family who shared their donated rice with a nearby Muslim neighbor, choosing not to hoard a gift when another was so in need.

In wisdom, she honored their charity by deciding not to quickly replenish their supply.

> *I didn't bring more rice that evening because*
> *I wanted them to enjoy the joy of sharing.*
>
> ———————————————————
>
> MOTHER TERESA OF CALCUTTA

Often, it takes tragedy to make us rise up with active compassion. Just moments after the horrific attacks on September 11, people across this land and throughout the world offered all they could—money, time, and countless good deeds—to desperate people in New York and Washington, D.C.

Similarly, during the holiday season, soup kitchens receive the bulk of their volunteers and donations. Yet hungry people use these charitable facilities year-round.

Although tragic events and holidays usually cause us to recall the needs of humanity, consider stepping outside your usual pattern and give to someone in need now.

Offer a warm smile and a helping hand, or if time doesn't permit and financial blessing is your gift, provide the funds needed so others can implement these gracious services in your place.

It's easy to get wrapped up in our own world—to wear blinders in some sense and not see the needs all around us.

If we are to emulate Christ, we must grasp on to the virtue of charity, the indwelling of love. Mother Teresa, who embraced this virtue above all others, compared our char- itable spirit to the giving nature of Christ.

Thoughtfulness is the beginning of great sanctity. If you learn the art of being thoughtful, you will become more and more Christ-like, for his heart was meek and he always thought of others. Our vocation, to be beautiful, must be full of thought for others.

MOTHER TERESA OF CALCUTTA

To whom do I reach out? you may wonder, especially if there are no hungry people in your neighborhood. Clearly, there are different levels of need, and many of them are right before us if we only open our eyes. Is someone you know going through a difficult divorce? Is it easier to turn away, not get involved, and hope the bad luck doesn't rub off on you? Or is it an act of love, compassion, and charity to show thoughtfulness toward your neighbor, offering an ear to listen, a warm hug, and a kind word in due time?

Sometimes the simplest act of kindness means the difference between a glimmer of light and ultimate darkness to a wounded soul. Jesus spoke of treating others the way we'd like to honor him. Amazing his followers, he explained that acts of charity toward others were, in reality, gifts to the Holy King.

For I was hungred, and ye gave me meat:

I was thirsty, and ye gave me drink: I was a stranger, and

ye took me in: Naked, and ye clothed me: I was sick, and ye visited

me: I was in prison, and ye came unto me. Then shall the righteous

answer him, saying, Lord, when saw we thee an hungred, and fed thee?

or thirsty, and gave thee drink? When saw we thee a stranger, and took

thee in? or naked, and clothed thee? Or when saw we thee sick, or in

prison, and came unto thee? And the King shall answer and say unto

them, Verily I say unto you. Inasmuch as ye have

done it unto one of the least of these my brethren,

ye have done it unto me.

_____

MATTHEW 25:35–40

Tell me, is your coworker exhausted, with three children, a full-time job, and an all-round high-stress life? Why not offer to watch her kids and purchase a gift certificate for a fabulous dinner so she and her husband can escape into a luxury they wouldn't think of giving themselves?

Although numerous virtues are mentioned in scripture, charity is elevated beyond the rest. Why? Because charity means love, the basis for all other virtues.

> *And now abideth faith, hope, charity, these three;*
> *but the greatest of these is charity.*

1 CORINTHIANS 13:13

How often do we become so spiritual, so pious that we feel we're above good deeds? "I will pray for you" is a wonderful statement, and praying is an act of love and compassion; however, what good is our faith without works to prove it true?

If my neighbor is hungry and I offer to pray for food but don't invite him to dinner, where is my true faith? Where is my compassion? Yes, there's no doubt that faith and works go hand in hand, for neither can exist without the other.

Remembering the Golden Rule (Do unto others as you would have them do unto you) is not just about being fair but about providing blessings, as well. Wouldn't you love to have someone watch your children and send you away for a romantic, quiet dinner with your spouse? Sure, we all would. Then why not offer someone else a gift you'd like to have? Yes, do unto others. Scripture is clear—we're not to become so "spiritual" that we forget to offer acts of kindness. Although we must pray and take time to meditate on scripture, gestures of love display the true signs of our faith. What doth it profit, my brethren, though a man say he hath faith, and have not works? Can faith save him?

If a brother or sister be naked, and destitute of daily food,
And one of you say unto them, Depart in peace, be ye warmed and
filled; notwithstanding ye give them not those things which are needful
to the body; what doth it profit? Even so faith, if it hath
not works, is dead, being alone.

JAMES 2:14–17

Note the scripture's intent. For here, in essence, is the balance to humanity:

> Thou shalt not avenge, nor bear any grudge
> against the children of thy people, but thou shalt love
> thy neighbor as thyself. . . .

———————————

LEVITICUS 19:18

Do not love your neighbor more than yourself, but do not hold yourself in higher esteem than another. A false sense of distorted humility, self-hatred, or self-abuse is not in the Lord's plan. You're a wonderful and amazing creation made in the very image of God. It's good to love yourself, just as he also does. Yet the flip side of this teaching is to love others in the same way you love yourself. No less. No more. How easy it is to look down on someone whose education or financial status is less than ours. How easy it is to make judgments about another's seemingly limited place in the world. In reality, however, they too are magnificent creations. The sooner we recognize who we are in God's eyes and offer others the love we want for ourselves, the sooner we'll understand the virtue of charity in its truest spiritual intent.

We've all heard the expressions "We reap what we sow" and "What goes around comes around." Have you ever found yourself in a horrible mood and lashing out at others, only to find your foul mood magically and unhappily reciprocated? On the other hand, have you ever approached strangers with a word of kindness or a simple compliment and been surprised at the positive response you received in return?

Last year, I experienced this phenomenon firsthand. As a writer, I have an innate desire to protect copyrighted material. I understand that although writing is an art and a joy, it is also a job. Yet for many people, copying someone's material and deleting the author's name is simply not considered stealing. After all, they presume, it's only art.

When a true Christmas story I'd written went out over the Internet, I looked forward to sharing it with others. It was December and a joyous holiday season. I wanted to give something of myself, without charge, as a present to strangers everywhere.

Within moments, I was blessed when I received volumes of wonderful e-mail. Much to my amazement, within a day, my story had made its way around the globe. Forward after forward it was sent, and person after person wrote back offering lovely words of appreciation.

I received greetings from individuals as far away as Europe, the Middle East, and Asia. As a writer, I was honored. As a person wishing to spread joy at Christmastime, I was humbled.

For days, responses came in, literally hundreds of e-mails from people touched by my simple Christmas story. Then, suddenly, everything began to spin out of control. A few readers had deleted my byline.

Before long, it was being forwarded as an anonymous story. Although some Webmasters had warned me this might happen, for the most part, I tried to ignore them. I figured, wasn't that just the downside of the Internet? I really didn't have control over the delete button of thousands of e-mailers, so why not just accept what was happening and trust God to handle it?

Then one night, I had enough. Exhausted and annoyed, I e-mailed the Webmaster of a site that had carried my story without author's credit.

I was mad. I felt pushed to the limit and decided to take it out on her. I decided I had to be strong, stand up for myself, and make sure she knew I was serious. I tried to sound tough (which I'm not), so I typed in the rudest tone I could muster that my story was copyrighted material and she did not have permission to use it.

I said it was nothing short of stealing to place it online and forward it to thousands of her subscribers without first doing a proper check on the author. I angrily signed my name, hit send, and went to bed.

The next morning, I woke up to over 100 new e-mails. Great, more fan mail, I thought. But as I began to open them up, one by one, it hit me. This wasn't fan mail at all, but angry, furious hate mail. As I pieced two and two together, I realized that in her frustration over my rudeness, she'd sent my e-mail out to her 4,000 subscribers. And let me tell you, several came after me with a vengeance.

At first, I felt defensive. After all, I wasn't the one who'd placed copyrighted material on the Internet and sent it out without first seeking the name of the author. I wasn't the person who'd done something wrong! But as time went on, the conviction in my spirit began to rise. There was no doubt about it—I was wrong, not in my premise but in my tone. Sure, copyrighted material is protected. Sure, authors deserve their bylines. I still believe that and always will.

Yet there are ways to handle things firmly but with kindness, and there are ways to inflict pain unnecessarily. Yes, she shouldn't have done it. Yes, she was wrong. But wasn't there a better way for me to handle the situation than by attacking her? By responding in anger before giving her a chance to correct the situation, I'd put her on the defense. And she chose to teach me a lesson. With a quick click and a send, she sent my angry words out to thousands of her readers, and they came back to haunt me later.

Person after person told me my original story had deeply touched their soul, but my e-mail had canceled all the prior good. They sensed hypocrisy and a cruel spirit, and they were deeply disappointed in me.

Clearly, they'd had me on a pedestal, and I'd fallen off. Wasn't I supposed to be more spiritual than that? (My family, by the way, laughs at the thought.) How could the woman who wrote this story also write such angry, rude words?

I was devastated. I cried nonstop. I didn't eat. I hardly slept. I felt the whole world hated me. And to make matters worse, I knew I'd hurt thousands of people, which was far from my original desire to share a loving story. It was Christmastime, no less (which many people pointed out by calling me Scrooge). Were their replies painful? Yes. But I knew they had a point.

One by one, I e-mailed each of them an apology. It took days, but I felt I owed them that much. Much to my amazement, most people responded with love. Oh, of course, a few remained annoyed. A few ignored me altogether. But the majority wrote back lovely notes of forgiveness, even including their own apologies for what they'd written to me.

They now understood firsthand how easy it was to get angry, write a nasty e-mail, and hit send before thinking it through. They understood from both sides of the fence that words can hurt.

They were sorry. I was sorry. Everybody was sorry. Lots of tears flowed from the United States to France and as far away as Nigeria.

What did I learn? Anger, hostility, and a nasty tone can wound people more than we can imagine. Words can be destructive. What's more, they'll all come back to bite the sender sooner or later.

And now? The story continues to circulate, especially over the holidays. However, when it includes my name, fine. When it appears without it, I ignore it or send a polite note asking the e-mail provider to update the file.

And much to my surprise, everyone has been more than agreeable. I could have saved myself—and thousands of people—pain that Christmas if I'd only chosen to embrace the spirit of charity, love, and kindness instead of attempting to rudely intimidate others out of my own desperation.

Without a doubt, each of us has an impact on our world. It may be positive; it may be negative, but when we choose to approach others with anger and bitterness, we spread animosity like wildfire. When we reach out in a loving way (although sometimes it must be firm), we are generally met with a similar response. We really do reap what we sow. Whether it's expressed with our words, our money, or our service, a spirit of kindness is essential to making this world a better place. The virtue of charity—tender acts of love, kindness, and compassion—will reach the very essence of God's heart, causing his light to shine forth for all to see.

Tips for Embracing
the Virtue of Charity

* Appreciate and love yourself. Yes, flaws and all. Remember, you're made in the very image of God and are a magnificent creation.

* Accept others as worthy of love. No one is perfect, but everyone has needs, hopes, and dreams. When you get right down to it, we're all more alike than different.

* Share a kind word, a prayer, a donation, your time, or your heart with someone who's hurting. Charity is more than prayers and desires—it's action.

* Remember the Golden Rule: Treat others the way you'd want to be treated. Freely offer forgiveness, kindness, and justice to others, believing that in time you'll reap what you sow.

* Offer a struggling individual a special gift of love, something you'd want someone to do for you.

JUSTICE

*No, no, we are not satisfied, and we will not be
satisfied until justice rolls down like waters and righteousness
like a mighty stream.*

MARTIN LUTHER KING, JR.

Justice—the virtue of expecting fairness for ourselves and
demanding it for others who cross our path. Justice mani-
fests itself in many forms. At times, it's simplistic—noticed
within human nature, even among the very young.
Imagine a group of small children playing at school. One is
being bullied, emotionally tossed about, for everyone to
see. Will the other children speak up and offer assistance

or turn and duck, hoping the bully doesn't come after them next?

Other times, justice is more complex. Are people within our hometown, our country, and even our world treated with basic human dignities, and if not, are we willing to reach out and address their needs? Tragically, countless individuals hiding in the false belief that they're not directly at risk often ignore human rights violations. If we're convinced we're safe from persecution, it is for some of us far easier to turn away than to come to the defense of those less fortunate. Yet there have been kind, brave souls, like the faithful family of Corrie ten Boom, who invited innocent and desperate Jewish individuals fleeing horrific Nazi persecution, with a secret place to hide. Yes, Corrie's courageous family members were willing to sacrifice their own safety in the desire to embrace the virtue of justice. What makes some people reach out and insure justice for others, even when they themselves are not directly under attack? Without a doubt, they cherish the virtue of justice, have a strong sense of right and wrong, and are ignited by the intense fire of compassion and love. Those who embrace the virtue of justice have a deep understanding of the Golden Rule. Even if they're not experiencing injustice themselves, they realize that someday they may be. If they don't speak up now and take action on an innocent person's behalf, who in the world will stand up for them when their need arises?

Years ago, my friend Laura worked in an environment where employees felt management was taking advantage of them through forced overtime and inadequate breaks. Tired and distraught, they were afraid to speak up for fear of losing their jobs. So, Laura, determined to seek justice, took the risk. Surprisingly, when she did, she found herself alone while all other voices remained silent. Although the room was filled with unhappy campers, she looked like the only dissenter. Yet when the meeting ended and management went about their business, countless colleagues told her how grateful they were that she'd spoken up. Amazing, isn't it? To protect themselves, they let my friend stand up for them all—alone. To add to this situation, weeks later, when another coworker was under pressure for refusing to work overtime, she practically begged Laura to come to her defense. If it were not so sad, it would have been funny. In the end, Laura did the right thing and chose to help the young girl, but how ironic it was that this person who'd remained silent in Laura's defense only weeks before now expected Laura to come to her rescue. Always remember—justice cuts both ways.

Those who embrace the virtue of justice have a deep understanding of basic human rights designed by our Creator and clearly see themselves as bound to take whatever steps are necessary to insure a higher moral outcome. How easy it is to stay silent, go about our business, look out for number one, and pretend injustice is simply not our problem. Yet scripture teaches us that we are to speak up for others because God is watching.

Open thy mouth, judge righteously, and
plead the cause of the poor and needy.

PROVERBS 31:9

Many people throughout history have risked their lives standing up to harsh regimes, only to cause great harm to themselves. They're passionately driven by an inner calling to seek justice at all costs. Scripture tells us that we're never to ignore the needs of others, even if the outcome doesn't directly impact our own safe, little world. By offering justice to the least fortunate, we have offered it to God himself.

Defend the poor and fatherless: do justice to the afflicted and needy.
Deliver the poor and needy: rid them out of the hand of the wicked.

PSALM 82:3–4

But is the oppressor always someone else? What if we're involved in a community, a government, or a doctrine that's treating others unfairly? Are we to stand up for the abused, make it right, and see that justice prevails? Scripture clearly reveals our answer.

We are fully accountable for how we treat others. God is watching. He that oppresseth the poor reproacheth his Maker: but he that honoureth him hath mercy on the poor.

PROVERBS 14:31

During the British imperial reign in India, Mahatma Gandhi experienced injustices at every turn. He didn't just speak up about government persecution. He also addressed a religious system that entrapped his own brothers, forcing them into lives of defeat simply because of a random chance of birth. Gandhi dealt with the injustice of the caste system as much as he addressed tyrannical government abuse. For he understood that justice must apply to everyone. He also grasped that persecution must be fought nonviolently, never allowing the victim to become the abuser himself.

The best way of losing a cause is to abuse your opponent and to trade upon his weakness.

MAHATMA GANDHI

Clearly, justice and charity go hand in hand. When we see someone suffering in an unfair situation and do not reach out to help that person, we've defied the very essence of love. Scripture shows that we're required to help those suffering from injustice and to lift others from darkness and despair, reaching out as their lifeline.

Learn to do well; seek judgment, relieve the oppressed, judge the fatherless, plead for the widow.

ISAIAH 1:17

How often, though, do we hear, "Their troubles aren't mine"? Of course, it's impossible for anyone to carry the burdens of the world upon his shoulders. Yet to ignore someone who's in need or being abused is in direct contrast to the sacred design for our lives. I love the passages of scripture where Jesus was approached about this very issue. The questioner tried to engage the Lord in a debate, to force him to specify exactly whom he was responsible for. Who is my neighbor anyway? Does the title literally apply to the man or woman next door, the person across town, or even a suffering individual on the other side of the globe? Just how far must we go to seek justice for others? Jesus made his answer clear in the story of the Good Samaritan. Interestingly, the Samaritans were not highly esteemed in their day. Yet of all the impressive people in the parable who marched coldly past the suffering individual, the Samaritan was the only one who understood the deeper meaning of justice. But he, willing to justify himself, said unto Jesus, "And who is my neighbour?"

And Jesus answering said, A certain man went down from Jerusalem to Jericho, and fell among thieves, which stripped him of his raiment, and wounded him, and departed, leaving him half dead. And by chance there came down a certain priest that way: and when he saw him, he passed by on the other side. And likewise a Levite, when he was at the place, came and looked on him, and passed by on the other side. But a certain Samaritan, as he journeyed, came where he was: and when he saw him, he had compassion on him, And went to him, and bound up his wounds, pouring in oil and wine, and set him on his own beast, and brought him to an inn, and took care of him. And on the morrow when he departed, he took out two pence, and gave them to the host, and said unto him, Take care of him; and whatsoever thou spendest more, when I come again, I will repay thee. Which now of these three, thinkest thou, was neighbour unto him that fell among the thieves?

LUKE 10:29–36

Are any of us really free unless everyone is? In a sense, aren't we all our brother's keeper? How often have you heard it said, "She was treated unjustly, but I can't complain because the tormentor never did anything wrong to me."

If we can't stand up for someone else, hoping to offer some element of justice, how can we expect anyone to stand up for us when our need arrives? Without a doubt, sooner or later our need will come. Listen to these wise words:

> *The love of justice is simply, in the majority*
> *of men, the fear of suffering injustice.*

FRANÇOIS, DUC DE LA ROCHEFOUCAULD

Yes, we must offer assistance to the abused, whether it's for the woman next door or an innocent child at school. We must insist that our voices be heard, even if theirs are too weak to be noticed. We must speak up for those whose cries of injustice have been drowned out by cruel dictators throughout the world.

For this is our sacred obligation. Abraham Lincoln, who dealt with the vast suffering caused by slavery and a nation torn in two, clearly understood the virtue of justice. He knew that without justice, true freedom would never exist.

Those who deny freedom to others, deserve it not for themselves;
and, under a just God, can not long retain it.

ABRAHAM LINCOLN

In more modern times, throughout the civil rights movement in the 1960s, many marched for justice, raising their banners high to insure equality for all God's children. Looking back, we realize how necessary the movement was.

Yet at the time, demonstrators were not only criticized but were also, in some cases, treated as criminals simply for speaking up for what was right. Though times have changed, injustice on different levels continues to rear its ugly head around the world.

By remembering that we're called to live by the Golden Rule, we can continue to reach out and insure that all people are promised the basic human dignity God intended us to enjoy. Abraham Lincoln understood that it would take more than rhetoric to bring ultimate justice to the people. It would take hard work, determination, and a clear grasp of right and wrong.

Why should there not be a patient confidence in the ultimate justice of the people? Is there any better or equal hope in the world?

ABRAHAM LINCOLN

Despite our desire to make things right, life can be unfair. Victims of crime and cruelty, who deserve the opportunity to receive their moment of healing, suffer greatly while they wait months, years, or in some cases forever to see justice prevail on their behalf.

Yet as a civilized culture, we understand the human need to hold criminals accountable while at the same time graciously insuring justice for them.

Although our legal system often brings about great frustration as we watch countless dollars, as well as time, spent trying a case, we can rest in the assurance that justice will prevail in the end. Legal counsel is provided for both sides, witnesses are intensely checked and verified, and through the best system we know, everyone is guaranteed an honest and fair trial.

But why does injustice occur at all? Why do the strong sometimes oppress the weak? Whether the oppressor is a cruel dictator, a violent criminal, a coworker who enjoys making you squirm, or a young bully on the playground, each strives to gain power by controlling another. In some cases, it's to attain great wealth; in other instances, it's simply done with the desire to make the abuser feel powerful.

Anytime someone is taken advantage of, we need to speak up, offer assistance, and make the situation right because injustice impacts us all.

If we examine our own lives, we may find that we're the ones taking advantage of others. Honestly ask yourself these questions:

- What exactly am I getting out of this situation?

- Is it worth it to bring another person down just to raise myself higher?

- Am I prepared to be accountable for the role I'm playing?

Let me challenge you to examine yourself.

When someone treats you unjustly, be courageous and speak up. But when you find you're the perpetrator, make amends quickly. Seek a better way.

Does God have a passion for justice? Of course he does. Our very hearts long for this virtue because we're created in his image. Think of Christ. He lived upon this earth during difficult times. The Romans were in control, desperately persecuting his people. There was trouble on every side.

Yet Christ came spiritually to free the captives. He had compassion for the injustices they suffered. Note the virtue of justice in the words of Christ:

> *The Spirit of the Lord is upon me, because he hath*
> *anointed me to preach the gospel to the poor; he hath sent*
> *me to heal the brokenhearted, to preach deliverance to the captives,*
> *and recovering of sight to the blind, to set at liberty them that*
> *are bruised, To preach the acceptable year of the Lord.*

LUKE 4:18–19

What, you may wonder, can you do today to contribute to an atmosphere of justice in your world? First, ask yourself these questions: Do I vote? Do I support the candidates who most stand for the positions I hold dear?

These may seem like obvious questions, yet astonishingly, many folks who clearly value justice never take the time to get involved in the basic political system. Holding on to the illusion that they are somehow insignificant in the larger scheme of life, they're simply not convinced they can honestly make a difference.

For the most part, these are good, caring people with sincere beliefs. However, by remaining uninvolved in the process, they indirectly contribute to the problem of injustice.

If you fit this description, if you haven't voted for years, take the time to become acquainted with the issues before you. Register to vote, and begin to make a difference in your community, your neighborhood, your country, and yes, even your world.

On a more spiritual note, begin to pray for justice. Ask God to infuse you with understanding, not just when you suffer wrong but also when others endure a similar plight. Never fear that prayer is useless or wasted time, for prayer is the beginning of any positive response. It will open your heart, your mind, and your spirit to the passion of God, filling you with the strength to pursue justice as the scripture commands.

To have our hearts in the right place to embrace the virtue of justice, we must first embrace the virtue of charity. For love inspires justice. When you observe suffering around you and offer your strength, your counsel, or a place of refuge, you've begun to make a small crack in the structure of cruelty. Your aid will not go unnoticed by the victim or our Creator.

By helping an abused woman, by lending counsel to a battered child, or by speaking up for someone whose tormentors will simply not let up, your passion for justice will successfully spill over into love. As the scripture reveals, we are to speak for the silent and lift up the weak, offering our strength in their place.

And the word of the Lord came unto Zechariah, saying,

Thus speaketh the Lord of hosts, saying, Execute true justice and

show mercy and compassion every man to his brother. And oppress not

the widow, nor the fatherless, the stranger, nor the poor; and let

none of you imagine evil against his brother in your heart.

ZECHARIAH 7:10

Without the virtue of justice, people are unable to see past their own needs. Pray for your eyes to be opened to injustices around you, and seek your part in making things right.

In so doing, the light of justice will shine upon your path, giving you the grace to continue on.

Tips for Embracing
the Virtue of Justice

* Look around you. Be aware of how others are treated. Make your world larger than your own family, your own town, or even your own country. Speak for those whose voices have been silenced.

* Live the Golden Rule. Even if it doesn't directly impact you, injustice, on any level, lowers the value of all human experience.

* Join a civic group that you particularly believe in. Write letters, make your voice heard, donate money, and see your world change for the better. Yes, you can make a difference!

* Vote, vote, vote! Stand up for the causes you believe in by voting for representatives who most support your positions. Yes, your vote does count.

* Pray for those who suffer injustice. Never believe prayer isn't active assistance. Prayer is an essential tool toward establishing justice.

* Examine your own life. If you find you're treating others unjustly, go to them quickly and make things right. We can't expect others to treat us fairly if we're not willing to do the same.

TEMPERANCE

I beseech you therefore, brethren, by the mercies of God,
that ye present your bodies a living sacrifice, holy, acceptable
unto God, which is your reasonable service.

ROMANS 12:1

Temperance—the virtue of self-control, to do all things in moderation.

Temperance may or may not imply sobriety, but it does encourage the ability to moderate our behavior not only with alcohol but also with overeating, overspending, overworking, or any other detrimental, excessive behavior. The virtue of temperance revolves around balance, which the Creator intended our lives to joyfully embrace. Freedom and temperance are close associates.

As long as we're slaves to our addictions, we can never truly be free. Instead of viewing temperance as bondage, forcing us to live up to a list of strict rules and regulations, view it as a gift, offering us the joyous lives we were designed to live.

Whatever your weakness or area of temptation, God is willing to substitute it with the virtue of temperance. Never believe the Creator is sending temptation your way; instead, realize his desire to replace your bondage with freedom. Scripture teaches us to embrace temperance in times of temptation.

Blessed is the man that endureth temptation:

for when he is tried, he shall receive the crown of life,

which the Lord hath promised to them that love him. Let no

man say when he is tempted, I am tempted of God: for God cannot

be tempted with evil, neither tempteth he any man:But every man is

tempted, when he is drawn away of his own lust, and enticed. Then

when lust hath conceived, it bringeth forth sin: and sin, when it is fin-

ished, bringeth forth death. Do not err, my beloved brethren. Every

good gift and every perfect gift is from above, and cometh

down from the Father of lights, with whom is no

variableness, neither shadow of turning.

JAMES 1:12–17

Jesus understands our temptations because on some level, he's experienced them, too, only without failure. Never be afraid to reach out in faith, fearing he'll shame you for your weakness. For scripture teaches that Christ is a compassionate and understanding high priest and that we should come without fear into his presence. Seeing then that we have a great high priest, that is passed into the heavens, Jesus the Son of God, let us hold fast our profession.

For we have not an high priest which cannot be touched with the feeling of our infirmities: but was in all points tempted like as we are, yet without sin. Let us therefore come boldly unto the throne of grace, that we may obtain mercy, and find grace to help in time of need.

HEBREWS 4:14–16

For many, an addiction to food is their ultimate downfall. Yes, this is a tough one. We just can't avoid food, give it up for Lent, and pretend it's a horrible temptation. We have to eat to survive.

So, how can we keep it in balance? Whether we eat doughnuts for breakfast, greasy burgers and fries for lunch, an entire pot roast for dinner, and every snack in between or virtually fast on the infamous Cabbage Soup Diet, the spirit of temperance calls us to make a different choice.

It calls us to a life of balance. For some, eating is all or nothing. I understand. I can fast with relative ease, but ask me to diet—to limit what I take in, to eat this but not that—well, look out, because trouble is on the way. If I have nothing to eat, I'm fine, but offer me a salad and you better not stand in the way of the entire chocolate cake.

Such behavior doesn't come without a price. Lack of energy, weight gain, and an unhealthy lifestyle have led me to embrace the spirit of temperance. Sure, overeating is an ongoing temptation, and I admit that it's sometimes difficult. Yet through prayer and sharing my struggle with others who've been down the same road, I'm seeing positive change.

The most successful nutritional programs encourage temperance by offering a variety of foods and teaching people to eat for fuel, as well as pleasure, but not to fill an emotional void or to eat merely for entertainment. Fit people seem to understand that managing food is neither about starvation nor gluttony, but about realistic moderation. They embrace the spirit of temperance and are living proof it's a virtue of divine design. Scripture teaches that our body is our temple, to be offered as a living sacrifice. Should we then doubt the Lord's desire to give the virtue of temperance to help us live a healthy life?

And be not conformed to this world: but be ye transformed by the renewing of your mind, that ye may prove what is that good, and acceptable, and perfect, will of God.

ROMANS 12:2

What about other excessive behaviors? For millions of people around the world, Alcoholics Anonymous has provided freedom from alcohol abuse. For those whose lives have been so devastated, a great service has been extended by this organization. Their support is incredible, and their success rate astonishing. Scripture clearly encourages the kind of support AA offers from one struggling individual to another.

Brethren, if a man be overtaken in a fault,

ye which are spiritual, restore such an one in the spirit of meekness;

considering thyself, lest thou also be tempted.

GALATIANS 6:1

Is it acceptable to drink in moderation? If your religion forbids it in any form, then by all means, follow your spiritual compass. But if you have no physical addiction to alcohol or religious stipulations forbidding its use, you fall into the vast majority of people. If alcohol doesn't take over your life and is merely a beverage of choice, it's likely you already possess the virtue of temperance.

If you have an addiction—whether to alcohol, medication, or cigarettes—don't be afraid to ask for help. Never be too proud. Call your doctor. Call a friend. And most of all, call on your Creator for the strength to make it through. Keep in mind that most people will not receive an instantaneous spiritual deliverance from their addictions (although this does happen), but know that if you seek medical help and emotional support and reach out to God in faith, you can overcome your addiction and embrace the virtue of temperance in your life once again.

For many, overspending is their Achilles' heel. This is my greatest temptation, my weakness—the area for which I most desire balance and temperance and continue to pray for strength. Oh, I'm getting better. But it took years of stress and flirting with financial disaster to help me curb my obsession with shopping. If you're struggling in this arena, use some logic besides prayer. Are you addicted to shopping? Then chances are you shouldn't hang out at the mall. Think about it: Alcoholics don't meet their friends in bars, do they? Would a serious dieter meander into a bakery, taking long whiffs of all the freshly made goods? Why put yourself through the temptation? Sure, your friends may shop, but maybe this isn't their area of weakness. At times, it will be necessary to go to the store; we can't avoid holiday shopping and buying school clothes. Yet we can work toward overcoming excessive spending on those and other occasions. Often, discovering the reasons why we get emotionally high from shopping is an important first step. Sometimes it takes hard, cold reality to wake us from denial. Unpaid bills or, worse yet, bankruptcy can bring a high-flying shopper back down to earth. But why let it get to that point?

Talking helps. Admitting you have a problem in the first place, quite frankly, takes some of the fun out of shopping and surprisingly curbs your obsession tremendously. My friend Tonya has a habit of keeping mail from her husband. Why? Because she's hiding a huge credit card bill she's convinced could harm her marriage. Amazingly enough, Tonya is still shopping. As crazy as it sounds, I understand her behavior completely. There were days I literally broke out in a cold sweat thinking about debt but moments later found myself at a mall buying who knows what and having a jolly good time, completely out of touch with reality.

One of my credit card companies offers an interesting service: a statement itemizing each purchase every customer makes for an entire year. The first time I received this nifty document, I nearly fell over. The page-by-page, blow-by-blow account folded out for what looked like two entire city blocks. I was mortified. Did they honestly think this was going to be helpful? Did they honestly think someone who shops as much as I do wants to be reminded of exactly where she's spent her money for an entire year?

Wiping the sweat from my brow, I threw the paper away—denial. Finally, talking it over with my spouse, who is not a spender, made change possible. And yes, I prayed. Believe me, I prayed. And you know what? I hardly crave the shopping experience anymore. What can I say? All the fun is gone. Now it's a practical thing that simply must be done on occasion. God has graciously given me the virtue of temperance, the gift of moderation regarding spending. I'm grateful beyond words, and so, of course, is my husband. Yet I'll never forget how easy it would be to slip back into addiction. Excessive indulgence goes far beyond the shopping mall. My friend Sharon recently bought a home. While applying for a mortgage, she heard a sermon on spending. Her minister implored, "Don't purchase an overly expensive house far beyond your reach just to impress others, or sure enough, your dream home will become your prison." Sharon took his advice, and although she qualified for a more extravagant house, she chose to live realistically within her means.

Meanwhile, Sharon has several friends with large, impressive homes that, just as her minister warned, have become their jail cells. Without the extra money to enjoy life, even to use the drive-up window at the local fast-food restaurant, they feel trapped inside their castles. Sharon's moderate spending habits, governed by the virtue of temperance, have allowed her to live a full existence filled with financial security, as she spends little time fretting over maintaining her lifestyle.

What about other obsessions? Will the virtue of temperance help in other ways? Of course it will. Do you border on being a workaholic? Are you convinced you're the only person who can get the job done right? Are you entrenched in work even when you're away from the office? Do you often bring stacks of papers home with you and then lock yourself away for hours from your loved ones? If you answer yes to these questions, chances are, you're addicted. Sure, we need to provide for ourselves and our loved ones. Sure, we need to be productive. No one admires a lazy person. But without temperance—without balance—our lives can easily spin out of control.

Learn to say no. Don't be shy, and for heaven's sake, don't feel guilty. Never take on more than you can comfortably accomplish. And here's a surprise: You're not the only person who can bake cookies for the troop, help out in the classroom, or organize that car wash. Get over the belief that if you don't do it, no one else will. After you move aside, others will step up to the plate. Saying no is also important for people working from home. With computers, fax machines, and pagers at our disposal, it's easy to accomplish most jobs without ever leaving the house.

However, as ideal as this working environment sounds, it's tempting to become trapped by addictive behavior. As a writer, I love working from my home. I'm near my children and able to schedule my life accordingly. But I'll never forget something my son, Nicholas, once said to me: "Mommy, you have less time for me now that you're home than when you went away to work." Ah, the wisdom of little ones. It's taken time, but I've learned to incorporate balance into my work schedule. Of course, that doesn't mean it's a goof-off family free-for-all. I'm only available for distraction during certain hours of the day. This is my office, and my work must be taken seriously. When I'm done, I resist the temptation (and let me promise you, it can be a temptation) to approach the computer and make just a few more quick changes. If I don't, I'll find myself lost for hours in my work, even though in theory I'm home so I can spend more time with my family.

Am I the only one who overworks? Absolutely not. My friend Tim is a talented and intelligent man. He's worked long and difficult hours climbing his way up the corporate ladder. Yet there's a certain sadness in his eyes, a sorrow reflecting a life that's nearly passed him by. His children are almost grown, and although he's a good father who's dedicated to his family, he missed much of what happened in their formative years. Yes, he's provided them with a lovely home and fabulous family vacations, but in the end, I'm not so sure they'd agree it was worth it. Ah, if he could just do it over again.

It's not just adults who become too busy. Even our kids can be overwhelmed with activities. After all, how many groups do our children really need to join? Between soccer, basketball, swimming, and scouting, your entire family could be on its way to a royal nervous breakdown.

Although I want my children to have full, productive lives, I also want them to understand the virtue of temperance, the value of moderation, in their day-to-day experience. I want them to appreciate the joy of leisure—to ride a bike, watch a movie, bake gooey peanut butter cookies, or sit in the sun and chat for hours with their new best friend. Like most people, I know tons of folks caught up in the soccer phenomenon. I'm sure it's a great sport that teaches children discipline, team spirit, and other good qualities, but for a family whose activity list is already 10 yards long, it can be enough to put the entire household right over the edge. When one enthusiastic soccer dad asked me why I refused to sign my kids up, I explained that they each had one group activity they'd already chosen to do.

My answer was simply not enough for him. Finally, after he implied that I was denying my children the joy they deserved, I got a little miffed. "Well," I said, "I didn't sign them up because I don't want my family's schedule to look anything like yours. It's Friday night, and your entire clan is getting up at 3:00 A.M. to drive across the state to a soccer game. You're exhausted, and I just don't want to join you in your frantic lifestyle."

What can I say? I haven't seen him since. Balance—it's all about balance.

To embrace the virtue of temperance, of moderation, does not mean that you or your kids have to stay home, sit around, and stare at each other. It just means you get off the vicious treadmill, and rejoin quality family life. Choose your activities wisely. Ask your kids to pick their favorite things to do, and consider limiting them to one or two at a time just a couple nights a week. Encourage them to play and to be creative without consistently needing an organization to call the shots. Encourage them to simply be kids and to embrace balance in their lives.

In the end, your exhausted family will thank you for it. Yes, slow down, take a deep breath, and evaluate your life. Where are you feeling out of balance? Where are you clearly out of control? Turn your weaknesses over to the Creator, asking him to infuse you with temperance in all areas of your existence, insuring a more balanced, healthy, and purposeful journey.

Tips for Embracing
the Virtue of Temperance

* Once you've discovered what your area of obsessive temptation is, admit it to yourself, then to someone else. Become accountable to that person when you fall into temptation.

* Consider joining a support group. Having others who share your area of weakness will help you feel you're not alone and lift you up in times of need.

* Examine all areas of your life. If alcohol or cigarettes are not your weakness, do you have other obsessive issues? Are you a workaholic, spendaholic, or even a foodaholic? Confront your area of weakness and begin to seek change.

* Pray for the virtue of temperance in all things. Ask for sacred strength. Recognize that temptation does not come from God. When you stumble (and we all do), ask for forgiveness, get back up, and move on. Never use past failures as an excuse to fail even more.

PRUDENCE

There is not a heart but has its moments of longing,
yearning for something better; nobler; holier than it knows now.

HENRY WARD BEECHER

Prudence—the virtue of wisdom, the divine ability to grasp solid, good judgments and make careful, clear decisions. How we all long for prudence. Have you ever had an important choice to make but been caught between two places or, worse yet, found yourself tossed about in a whirlwind of indecision? Well, we can rest in the assurance that even though our minds are limited in understanding, we can ask for divine assistance. It's our right as believers.

And although it may be hard to comprehend, God longs to share his knowledge with us, even more than we seek to discover it. Those promises are ever true, just as much today as thousands of years ago.

So why do we continue to struggle, stumbling down a dimly lit path with limited understanding when a well-lit road is available simply for the asking? If we can step outside our pride and seek guidance and wisdom, life's journey will take on new meaning, purpose, and design. Look at the scriptural assurance urging us to seek prudence in times of need:

For I will give you a mouth and wisdom, which
all your adversaries shall not be able to gainsay nor resist.

LUKE 21:15

Have you ever felt that life has ganged up on you, that you have enemies on every side, and that there is nowhere to turn—no answer to free you from your dilemma? Instead of fretting, ask God for wisdom, for divine guidance, and for the perfect words, spoken at just the right moment. Ultimately, it can't be planned out, schemed out, or practiced for hours in front of a mirror. When the virtue of prudence arrives and you speak to your adversaries, even you'll be amazed at how effective you are. "Okay," you say, "that was fine for those Bible folks walking around in long, bulky robes thousands of years ago. But what about today? What about my life? Is divine wisdom still available to me just for the asking? Of course it is. God's promises hold true even now. To better illustrate this point, I'd like to share a true story about my friend Cindy, who by the virtue of prudence was able to comprehend a seemingly senseless situation.

Cindy is a lovely woman with a giving heart. Her desire to help children molded her future. It brought her through college as she studied special education and helps her today as she diligently teaches in the field. Cindy's prayer was clear from the beginning—that through her strength, she would make a difference, reach out to children in need, and lighten their heavy loads. Even with dreams born of love and a heart full of prayers, life isn't easy. Last year, a menacing spider crossed Cindy's leg. She panicked, leaped into the air, landed wrong, and promptly broke her foot.

It was a painful injury, yet one her doctor promised would soon heal. But he was wrong. As the weeks turned into months, Cindy began to wonder, Why am I still hurting? Why did I have this accident in the first place? Why must I depend on others to do the simple tasks I once took for granted? Cindy cried out to God for wisdom, but her prayers went unanswered—that is, until one day when he spoke.

Nine-year-old Mark had cerebral palsy. He was a shy child, who rarely spoke to anyone, and walked with the assistance of an awkward, heavy brace. Although he was assigned to another teacher, Cindy watched him from afar. One afternoon, several classes gathered together in a circle. Cindy limped in, frustrated, almost fuming from the limitations of her temporary handicap, and sat down beside him.

Mark didn't speak a word, but the following day, he sent her a note. The moment she opened it, her eyes filled with tears. After enduring months of heavenly silence, Cindy finally understood why she had struggled so long, why her limp had refused to go away, and why God had postponed answering one prayer in order to respond more deeply to another. In the end, her weakness, not her strength, had finally allowed her to made a difference, reach out to a child in need, and lighten his heavy load. The note? It simply read:

Dear Cindy,
You are nice. You are pretty. I like you
because you walk just like me.
Your friend,
Mark

Surely the gift of wisdom is available for the asking. Although we aren't capable of grasping the full spectrum of God's purpose, opening our hearts and minds with humility and prayer can impart insight beyond our expectations. How much easier will life's journey be if we look away from our circumstances and from what seems unanswerable and simply ask for divine wisdom? Hear the prayer of David as he sought the virtue of prudence:

Let my cry come near before thee, O Lord:
give me understanding according to thy word.

––––––––––––––

PSALM 119:169

First, consider this: Do you really want divine guidance? Do you really want true wisdom? I ask, because as humans, we often request what we really don't desire. Have you ever heard the expression "Be careful what you pray for because you just might get it?" I can't tell you how many times I've asked for wisdom, only to receive it and then promptly run screaming for the hills. "Not that answer. I thought you'd tell me what I wanted to hear." When we're in a place where we really believe God knows best and are willing to apply what we've learned, he will be ready to send wisdom our way. When we ask with all our hearts, all our sincerity, and not just in casual passing, we'll be surprised at how quickly the answer comes. Why should we continue to take on challenges and make detailed plans for our lives without asking for divine intervention? Grab hold of this wise counsel:

Never undertake anything for which you wouldn't have the courage to ask the blessing of heaven.

G. C. LICHTENBERG

Note the intense desire necessary to fully embrace this blessing. Scripture teaches us to seek the virtue of prudence with all our might. We're told to seek it like a priceless fortune. We're not to take this gift lightly or ask for it as an afterthought but to search for it diligently, like a hidden treasure.

My son, if thou wilt receive my words, and hide my commandments with thee; So that thou incline thine ear unto wisdom, and apply thine heart to understanding; Yea, if thou criest after knowledge, and liftest up thy voice for understanding; If thou seekest her as silver, and searchest for her as for hid treasures; Then shalt thou understand the fear of the Lord, and find the knowledge of God. For the Lord giveth wisdom: out of his mouth cometh knowledge and understanding.

PROVERBS 2:1–6

What's more, when you ask for wisdom, believe it will be offered. How often do we ask for help and then doubt it's on the way? How often do we hear the truth and then question if it's really our answer? Reach out in faith, not in fear, and discover the gifts you'll receive. The scripture teaches us not to analyze things until we come up with the answer but to ask God for truth.

If any of you lack wisdom, let him ask of God, that giveth
to all men liberally, and upbraideth not; and it shall be given him.
But let him ask in faith, nothing wavering. For he that wavereth
is like a wave of the sea driven with the wind and tossed.

JAMES 1:5–6

Now, I know that we've all heard about people who, believing they'd heard from God, acted out in bizarre and even dangerous ways. Such stories can leave us afraid to seek the virtue of prudence. But true wisdom will never do harm to anyone. It will not have you take your life in exchange for a ride on the Hale-Bopp comet, nor will it have you do anything outside God's higher moral law. If you're hearing these sorts of whispers, they're not coming from the Creator. Remember, true wisdom is always good, always pure, and always in line with what's moral and right. Scripture gives us solid groundwork for recognizing the true source of knowledge.

But the wisdom that is from above is first pure,

then peaceable, gentle, and easy to be intreated, full of mercy and good

fruits, without partiality, and without hypocrisy.

JAMES 3:17

Do you feel there's no need for divine wisdom? Are you a practical-minded person, so sure you can figure it all out on your own? I understand. At times, life is meant to work that way. After all, we've been given certain gifts already— our minds and the ability to reason much out on our own. These are attributes that should never be discouraged. God gave us each a brain and certainly expects us to use it. No one needs to ask God if he should feed his children or get a job to earn an honest living. Some things are just blatantly obvious. However, there are times when all the reasoning in the world, all the study, and all the tuning in and concentration will not bring you the answers you so desperately need. It's then that the cry for divine wisdom will rise up within you, as your soul reaches out for far more than mortal man can offer. Scripture makes it clear—the virtue of prudence will edify our lives, bringing honor into our existence. Get wisdom, get understanding: forget it not; neither decline from the words of my mouth.

Forsake her not, and she shall preserve thee: love her, and she shall keep thee. Wisdom is the principal thing: therefore get wisdom: and with all thy getting get understanding. Exalt her, and she shall promote thee: she shall bring thee to honour, when thou dost embrace her. She shall give to thine head an ornament of grace: a crown of glory shall she deliver to thee.

PROVERBS 4:5–9

To better illustrate the need for wisdom in our lives, let me share a true experience. While working at a local hospital a few years ago, I had to rush away from my desk to use the rest room. It was a busy night in the emergency room, so I quickly excused myself and dashed down the hall toward the nearest bathroom. As I approached the familiar door, I felt an intense inner warning, "Don't go in there. Go to the next rest room instead." Although the thought was clear, authoritative, and persistent, I argued with that still, small voice: "I don't have time to chase down the hallway in search of another rest room. I'm in a hurry, and there's nothing wrong with the one right in front of me." Insistent and sure I was making a sound decision, I opened the door and went in (but only after checking to make sure everything appeared safe). Despite the warning, things seemed to go off without a hitch. I found myself giggling at the ridiculous message as I washed and dried my hands. But then, just as my smirking reached its peak, I glanced over to see the water in the flushing toilet rise up and begin to overflow. I couldn't believe it. I didn't know whether to laugh, cry, or run. After not finding a gauge to turn off the tide, I chose to run. As I quickly made my way down the hall, I glanced back to discover a river trailing closely behind me. A cry for help went out, and before long, after a visit from the janitor, all was dry again. However, I was still shaken, not knowing quite what to make of it all.

Confused, I shared my story with my coworker. Why in the world, I wondered, would God give me such a strange warning? Some people, I reasoned, get important messages from God, even divine inspiration. They are called to the mission field, called to save lives by opening a desperately needed orphanage. I, on the other hand, got the toilet call. What was that all about, and what in the world did it say about who I was? If God desired to share something with me and the very secrets of the universe were a possibility, why would he entrust me with such a silly word like this? Just then, my coworker (who was not known for having a particularly spiritual side) began to speak volumes of wisdom. "Candy," she whispered between laughter, "if you don't listen to God in the small things, why should he tell you anything more important?" Bingo. I got the message—loud and clear. Don't just ask. Listen.

So how does God speak to us? I can almost hear you ask. It can happen in various ways. Perhaps you'll read scripture and the very answer to your modern-day problem will seem to jump off the page. Perhaps a friend will approach you with exactly the right words at exactly the right moment without being prompted. Sometimes our very intuition is used to hear the still, small voice of God. Whether it warns us of danger, of the direction for our pathway, whom to marry (or whom not to), where to attend school, which job to take, or even which bathroom to enter, we should always honor wisdom. Yes, if we don't listen to God in the small things, why should we expect him to reveal anything more?

Humility is necessary to receive the virtue of prudence. We must be able to let go of our own overconfidence; trusting God's judgment is better. It isn't always easy. But don't let ego, pride, and just plain embarrassment cause you to miss out on divine wisdom. Scripture reveals that our wisdom is limited when we look at the larger spectrum. Only God can shed true light on our circumstances, revealing divine wisdom from above.

Let no man deceive himself. If any man among you seemeth
to be wise in this world, let him become a fool, that he may be wise.
For the wisdom of this world is foolishness with God . . . .

1 CORINTHIANS 3:18–19

King Solomon, held in high esteem for his vast wisdom, wasn't born with this great gift but searched the heavens to discover it. Imagine this: Solomon was young and afraid. Every task before him seemed overwhelming and beyond his comprehension. No, King Solomon did not have an inferiority complex; he was simply a realist. In truth, he was in over his head. Yet with the proper perspective and humility, he knew the one who was able to infuse him with wise judgments, the one who knew the right way to go and exactly which way to turn. I can't help but love Solomon. Just like most of us, he often felt overwhelmed, incapable, and hungry for divine answers. And his heartfelt prayer, capable of reaching through the ages, moved the very hand of God:

And now, O Lord my God, thou hast made thy servant king instead of David my father: and I am but a little child: I know not how to go out or come in. Give therefore thy servant an understanding heart to judge thy people, that I may discern between good and bad: for who is able to judge this thy so great a people? And the speech pleased the Lord, that Solomon had asked this thing. And God said unto him, Because thou hast asked this thing, and hast not asked for thyself long life; neither hast asked riches for thyself, nor hast asked the life of thine enemies; but hast asked for thyself understanding to discern judgment; Behold, I have done according to thy words: lo, I have given thee a wise and an understanding heart; so that there was none like thee before thee, neither after thee shall any arise like unto thee. And I have also given thee that which thou hast not asked, both riches, and honour: so that there shall not be any among the kings like unto thee all thy days.

----

1 KINGS 3:7 AND 9–13

Sound easy enough? Solomon's humility, his ability to honestly admit his own inadequacies and recognize God's awesome possibilities, made his prayer able to be heard on high.

Notice that King Solomon didn't ask for personal favors. He didn't ask for wealth. (Have you ever prayed to hit the lottery? Well, join the crowd.) He didn't ask for God to get his enemies; he asked for wisdom to do the job set before him—to fully live the life he was given. And God heard and honored him abundantly. In fact, God tossed in great personal wealth as a bonus.

Remember the story of Solomon and the two babies? The desperate mothers stood frantically before him. One child had died; the other was still alive. Both women claimed the living infant as theirs.

Now, as you know, this was thousands of years ago. There was no DNA testing to prove who was telling the truth. This was a desperate case calling for divine wisdom.

Let's see how the gift of prudence helped Solomon respond:

> And the king said, Bring me a sword. And they brought a sword before the king. And the king said, Divide the living child in two, and give half to the one, and half to the other. Then spake the woman whose the living child was unto the king, for her bowels yearned upon her son, and she said, O my lord, give her the living child, and in no wise slay it. But the other said, Let it be neither mine nor thine, but divide it. Then the king answered and said, Give her the living child, and in no wise slay it: she is the mother thereof.

I KINGS 3:24–27

Ah, the wisdom of Solomon. Just as the scripture promised, he is known even to this day as a great king of infinite judgment.

And all he did was ask.

Tips for Embracing
the Virtue of Prudence

* Ask in faith. Believe that when you ask for wisdom, divine answers will come your way. Be open to the method by which they may arrive. It may be different than what you expect.

* Have pure motives (remember King Solomon). If your heart is to serve God better, your prayers will be honored.

* Be certain the wisdom you're receiving is divinely inspired. Ask yourself, Is this insight positive? Will it ultimately bless others? Does it harmonize with scripture?

* Trust wisdom, even if it doesn't seem to make sense at the time.

* Listen to your inner voice. It's often the still, small voice of God speaking to your heart. Your instincts are divine tools. Use them.

* Act on what you've been shown. If you consistently reject small grains of wisdom, you can't ever expect to receive more.

FORTITUDE

...the trying of your faith worketh patience. But let patience
have her perfect work, that ye may be perfect
and entire, wanting nothing.

———————

JAMES 1:3–4

Fortitude—the virtue of perseverance, to endure sometimes difficult circumstances with the sheer determination
to see your dreams come to pass. It's so easy to give up too
quickly, whether we're struggling to learn a new skill, to
stay faithfully on a diet, to get through difficult financial
times, to endure catastrophic personal events, or to work
diligently, while waiting endlessly, to see our dreams come

true. My friend Rosie is gifted with the virtue of fortitude. She's a creative, talented, and impressive writer, but she's never for a moment rested on her natural abilities. Instead, Rosie has honed her craft and studied the business. She is always open to suggestion and, most important, continues to practice her writing skills daily. Rosie's dream is to see her manuscript be published or her screenplay come to life in the theater.

Most aspiring writers can relate. Although she's submitted numerous queries for her work and often received favorable reviews, time after time she's been given the devastating, disappointing blow of ultimate rejection.

Oh, Rosie understands it's not personal. Publishing is a business, and many factors, besides talent, come into play. Yet she continues to try, to endure, and to faithfully wait for her one, big break. And I believe in time that break will come. It's bound to because Rosie embraces the virtue of fortitude deeply within her life, never making shallow attempts at half-thought-out plans in the hope that in the end they will work out. Sheer determination and perseverance indwell her spirit. Although Rosie has loyal people who support her dream, she also has her fair share of folks who enjoy bringing her down. (Don't we all?) You know, the people who love to poke at others' dreams, smirk at their failures, and bring up the many years they've waited with little to show for their trouble.

I have no doubt that when her reward finally comes, when her success explodes on a grand, wonderful scale, some of those very same people will applaud the loudest, pretending they've supported her all along.

Yes, Rosie's life reflects the virtue of fortitude. And she continues to walk forward, waiting and hoping for her final reward.

I love what Abraham Lincoln said about the virtue of fortitude. He clearly understood that hard work, determination, and perseverance were vital for success.

Every man is proud of what he does well; and

no man is proud of what he does not do well. With the former,

his heart is in his work; and he will do twice as much of it with less

fatigue. The latter performs a little imperfectly, looks at it in disgust,

turns from it, and imagines himself exceedingly tired. The little

he has done comes to nothing, for want of finishing.

ABRAHAM LINCOLN

American immigrants, especially, grasp the virtue of fortitude on an intrinsic level. Many, having come from poverty, hold tightly to their faith in the American dream. They know that anyone can be a success in this country if they work hard and believe it can truly happen. Amazingly enough, because of their faith and discipline, it often does. My husband came to the United States from Fiji in 1982. Like most immigrants, he was poor but held tightly to his dreams. Sure, there were hardships, but without them, how would he ever learn to persevere? When he first settled in California, he walked from business to business, seeking employment, any employment. He was willing to do anything—wash dishes, sweep floors, pump gas; you name it. This man wasn't too proud for work. But much to his dismay, no one wanted to hire him. By the end of the day, exhausted and wet from a sudden cloudburst, he boarded a public bus, placing his last bit of change in the meter. When he sat down, virtually alone, he discovered a dollar bill on the empty seat next to him. It was the last dollar he had in the world. To this day, my husband gets misty-eyed when he shares that story. Yes, his circumstances were humbling. Yes, they were difficult. But they also made him more determined to succeed. Within a few days, he found a job pumping gas and worked diligently hour upon hour, all the while holding on to a bigger dream growing in his heart. Before long, he put himself through school, became a citizen, married me, and had two children. Eventually, he landed a better job, then a better one, and now he happily works as a manager for a private foundation. He did it all without ever taking a dime of public assistance.

A couple of years ago, we were able to buy our dream home in a lovely community surrounded by private lakes, abundant wildlife, majestic oaks, and spectacular golf courses. Soon after our move, while out on a stroll, I leaned over to my husband and said, "Pinch me. Can you believe we live in such an incredible place? Can you believe we're actually here?" Calmly and with the assurance of someone who grasps the virtue of fortitude, he confidently said, "Of course I believe it. I always knew it would happen." Thinking he misunderstood me, I rephrased my question. "Are you trying to tell me that when you were a new immigrant, you actually believed you'd someday own a home in a community as wonderful as this?" "Yes," he said firmly, "I always knew if I worked hard, prayed hard, and waited long enough, this was all possible."

Ah, the fortitude of an immigrant not jaded by years of disappointment but still warmed by the fire of the American dream. People other than immigrants have embraced the virtue of fortitude. Think about the soldiers who've endured unbelievable suffering and fear with the goal of safely returning home from a successful mission.

In the Second World War, the soldiers were not assigned a limited tour of duty. They were there for the duration, whatever that turned out to be. They came back either wounded, in a coffin, or victoriously alive when the war was won. Talk about a reason to win a war: Because of their desire to return home safely, World War II was decided in record time.

My dad was a young man, barely twenty, when he signed up for duty. On the long flight destined for an American base in China, he listened only halfheartedly to instructions regarding crash procedures. After all, he was headed off to war. Why worry right then? It just didn't seem important. After the war ended, however, and he was ready to come home, he viewed things far differently. Suddenly, the will to persevere—the spirit of fortitude—took over every fiber of his being. Now nothing would stop him from returning home safely. Motivated by the goal to get back to his loved ones, he was suddenly filled with determination. On the first of three separate flights en route to his town, he paid attention to every last detailed instruction, even locating his parachute on the wall and staring at it for the majority of the trip, just in case he needed it. On the second flight, he took the chute off the wall and placed it under his seat for safekeeping. And on the third flight, as he was approaching his final destination, he lifted his parachute off the seat and put it on!

To embrace the virtue of fortitude, we first need a reason, something to motivate our spirit; then we must have the faith to believe our goal is truly possible. Most of all, we must act—do our part to make our dreams come true. Without difficulty, there would be no need for perseverance. Without perseverance, there'd be no opportunity to learn patience. They all go together.

What part does prayer play in the virtue of fortitude? In scripture, we're taught never to give up on prayer but to persevere, to endure, to continue to ask. Yes, even in prayer the virtue of fortitude is honored. One day, Jesus shared a story with his disciples, instructing them never to give up in life or in prayer:

> And he spake a parable unto them to this end, that men ought always to pray, and not to faint; Saying, There was in a city a judge, which feared not God, neither regarded man: And there was a widow in that city; and she came unto him, saying, Avenge me of mine adversary. And he would not for a while: but afterward he said within himself, Though I fear not God, nor regard man; Yet because this widow troubleth me, I will avenge her, lest by her continual coming she weary me. And the Lord said, Hear what the unjust judge saith. And shall not God avenge his own elect, which cry day and night unto him, though he bear long with them? I tell you that he will avenge them speedily. . . .

LUKE 18:1–8

Does God himself have a persistent nature? Yes, and he is our example. Look at what scripture says about the way he honors fortitude. When we're feeling weak and tempted to give up, he will lift us up. All we must do is ask. Hast thou not known? Hast thou not heard, that the everlasting God, the Lord, the Creator of the ends of the earth fainteth not, neither is weary? There is no searching of his understanding. He giveth power to the faint, and to them that have no might he increaseth strength. Even the youths shall faint and be weary, and the young men shall utterly fall:

But they that wait upon the Lord shall renew their strength;
they shall mount up with wings as eagles; they shall run, and not be
weary; and they shall walk, and not faint.

ISAIAH 40:28–31

What about those working for social justice? How much of a role do fortitude, patience, endurance, hard work, and determination play in creating positive social change? Fortitude is vital to the very core of such progress. Clearly, little happens overnight, especially not drastic, necessary social change. This country owes a great deal to Martin

Luther King Jr., who understood that his calling, his vision, and his goals were never going to be accomplished by a quick fix. The fulfillment of this vision would take decades of intense work propelled by those who understood the virtue of fortitude, people who never gave up nor lost sight of the ultimate dream.

And as we walk, we must make the pledge that we shall always march ahead. We cannot turn back.

MARTIN LUTHER KING JR.

How many of us have difficulty sticking to our individual dreams? For example, how many diets have we struggled with in the last five years? How do some of us manage to obtain the virtue of fortitude throughout the long and sometimes difficult weight-loss process? Why is it that one person will give in to the temptation of chocolate cheese-cake, whereas another will resist the same delight? Some call it willpower. Some call it sheer determination, but as long as the virtue of fortitude is present, the human spirit is capable of enduring and persisting in amazing ways. The next time you set a goal, imagine the results clearly. Can you get a picture of yourself thinner, healthier, and looking and feeling great? For some, this vision is difficult to conjure up. When our self-image is distorted by negative thoughts, it's hard to see past the person in the mirror. If your imagination is limited, try cutting out pictures of healthy, slim body types from magazines and placing them around the house. But please refrain from torturing yourself with photos reflecting the airbrushed perfection of supermodels. Instead, find someone with a similar height, age, and look as yours, minus the excess pounds. Now, post that image on your bedroom mirror. Instead of thinking of yourself as a heavy person trying to lose weight, imagine yourself already slender, healthy, and active. When you see yourself in this way, you will be more likely to eat appropriately and, in turn, shed excess weight.

A friend of mine lost extra pounds by using this method. She called it "thinking thin." Soon after her husband noticed her drastic physical change, he asked what she was doing to realize her goals. She began to explain that by visualizing herself as already thin, she simply wanted to eat less. Only half listening, he began to ponder the concept.

One afternoon, while serving himself a giant bowl of ice cream, he proclaimed he was trying her new diet. "Then why," she asked, "are you eating so much ice cream?" "I'm thinking thin," he replied. Then he began to repeat out loud, "This will not make me fat. This will not make me fat." In a fit of laughter, she explained that he'd missed her point entirely. Visualization is not magic. Those calories still exist. If her husband's mind had been fixed on believing his goal was already a reality, he wouldn't have craved the ice cream in the first place. If you pursue with all your might what you believe to be true and live out in your mind, then it can become reality. It's all part of the virtue of fortitude.

Do the same principles apply to career goals? Sure they do. Start by writing your dreams down. Where would you like to be in five years, ten years, twenty-five years? What do you think it will realistically take to get you there? Do you need to go back to school? Do you need to take a new job, a risk, to put you in the right place for advancement? Once you've made up your mind about what your dream is and what steps you will take to achieve it, begin to lift your faith.

Read material that supports your goals. Devour success stories from people who've lived your dream, and begin to dream right along with them. Pray for the fortitude to follow your plan and begin a brighter future filled with hope.

Yes, your circumstances may be difficult, but imagining, believing, praying, and working diligently toward those goals are the very tools that support fortitude. You have to start sometime. Why not now?

Tips for Embracing
the Virtue of Fortitude

* Once you've discovered your dream and determined your goal, begin to pursue it with all your might. What must you do first? Take it step by step. Do you need to better your education, find a mentor, or simply work harder at your job? Whatever it takes, make the decision to sacrifice, and keep on going until you see your dream come true.

* When times are difficult, realize you can pray for the virtue of fortitude to bring you through, even when every fiber in your being cries out that you should give up. Remember, God will give you the strength to go on.

* Be persistent in prayer. Clearly, fortitude is honored in scripture as a desired method of approaching God with our needs.

* Read about others who've lived your dream. How did they endure difficult times? As you absorb their step-by-step process, their spirit of fortitude will inspire you.

FAITH

*Nobody seriously believes the universe was made
by God without being persuaded that He takes care of His works.*

———————————

JOHN CALVIN

Faith—the virtue of believing and trusting in what's often unseen, the assurance that even though all can't be reasoned out, there is a higher plan, a purpose, and a destination for goodness.

Sometimes our faith is strong, whereas other times it feels weak, scattered, or even absent altogether. There are days when we struggle to believe anything good can come of our lives or our difficult circumstances. Yet each of us is given a measure of faith. And the tiniest drop of faith is a powerful force.

The scripture speaks volumes on faith.
For we walk by faith, not by sight.

---

2 CORINTHIANS 5:7

In scripture, we're told that Christ's followers felt inadequate at times, asking Jesus for more faith to do the work set before them. They were firmly reassured that the measure they were already given was all they really needed.

And the apostles said unto the Lord, Increase our faith.
And the Lord said, If ye had faith as a grain of mustard seed, ye
might say unto this sycamine tree, Be thou plucked up by the root,
and be thou planted in the sea; and it should obey you.

LUKE 17:5–6

Imagine that. No special formulas required. No magic mantras, no deep-breathing techniques, no bargaining—only simple faith and asking in line with God's ultimate plan.

We need just a tiny grain of faith to reach out, pray unselfishly, and genuinely seek the will of God. Our part is small. God will do the rest. Scripture teaches us the important role persistence plays in faith. Ask, and it shall be given you; seek, and ye shall find; knock, and it shall be opened unto you:

For every one that asketh receiveth; and he that seeketh findeth; and to him that knocketh it shall be opened.

MATTHEW 7:7–8

What are your needs? Are you lonely, out of work, out of money, or all of the above and more? Although God already knows the details, part of faith is sharing a relationship with our unseen Creator.

Open up your heart and share your fears, your tears, and your hopes and dreams. Don't bother trying to sound spiritual. He's not impressed. Forget the thees and thous. God understands modern English. Don't attempt to hide the ugly details. He already knows. And what's more, he still loves you. Just get it out there on the table and then let the Creator work.

Now here's the tricky part. Hold back your natural inclination to offer God solutions. He really doesn't need your advice. I can't tell you how many times my prayers have been riddled by prefabricated bonus answers.

"Here's my problem, God. Now here are your choices. You can either do A, B, or C. Thanks and amen."

Sure enough, every time, God ignores my advice and does X, Y, or Z. Yet much to my amazement, his ways are always best.

Think of your grasp for faith as an opportunity to discover a plan that may have completely eluded you—another door, a way out of your circumstances that you may have never otherwise considered. Then hold on to faith as you await your answer.

Most of us have prayed for something that didn't come to pass. Perhaps our desire was not in our best interest, even though we thought it was at the time. Or perhaps it was a prayer born of selfishness. Scripture reveals why some prayers are denied.

> *Ye lust, and have not: ye kill, and desire to*
> *have, and cannot obtain: ye fight and war, yet ye have not,*
> *because ye ask not. Ye ask, and receive not, because ye ask*
> *amiss, that ye may consume it upon your lusts.*

———————

JAMES 4:2–3

Even today, we still manage to get hung up on being told no. I remember when years ago a college English professor took time out from the first day of class to attack any student who held their faith dear. Out of the blue and without bearing on the subject at hand, he began to tell a story from his childhood. As a young boy, he sincerely wanted his baseball team to win, so he prayed faithfully for such an outcome. But sure enough, his team lost. From that day on, he doubted the very existence of God and gleefully challenged anyone who felt differently. How sad. This seemingly insignificant event had a huge impact on his life, most obviously, because he was still bringing it up many years later and on the first day of English class, no less.

Clearly, his prayer was one of difficult reasoning. Sure, God cares about the little things in our lives. But praying to win a baseball game certainly runs the risk of being considered amiss (and of course there's the obvious dilemma of people praying for opposite teams). After all those years, this man still hadn't gotten over his disappointment in God's not jumping through his hoop. It seemed he was still having a tantrum more than thirty years later because the Lord of the Universe had the audacity to tell him no.

But what if our prayer is sincere, not selfish, and seems to have all the right elements for an affirmative answer yet our request is denied anyway? This challenge is far more difficult to grapple with. After all, why would a sincere prayer, uttered in faith and appearing to be for the greater good, ever be denied? This is a question humanity has always wrestled with.

Years ago, my only sibling, Spring, was diagnosed with terminal brain cancer. She was twenty-one, and I was only seventeen. Despite hearing dire medical evaluations, I was convinced that she would be healed. How did I know this to be so? I was certain because I believed the scripture of the mustard seed. I knew God could do all things

. . . With men this is impossible; but with
God all things are possible.

MATTHEW 19:26

Certainly, if I did my part by praying in faith, God would be obligated to do his. He would move mountains for my family. My prayer was not selfish; it was sincere and filled with faith and confidence in God's power, love, and abilities. So how could it possibly be denied?

Day by day, my sister continued to grow worse, yet my faith rarely faltered. I would see a miracle. Of this, I was sure. But within a year, despite my faith-filled prayers, my sister tragically died. My reaction went far beyond grief to utter shock. Although the doctors had made it clear all along that there was no hope, I knew I was dealing with the Great Spiritual Physician. Didn't he have a promise to keep?

Following Spring's death, I withdrew spiritually for almost five years. What was the point in having faith? Oh, I still believed God was real, and I still believed he was powerful enough to do anything, including heal cancer. Yet I was grappling with the fact that he chose not to. I wasn't doubting God's reality; I was doubting his goodness.

Through it all, he was gracious and patient with me.

Eventually, I came to terms with my limited understanding of divine will and purpose. I realized scripture needed to be taken in its entirety, not portion by portion. Clearly, I still believe that God holds the ultimate control in his hands. His will was simply different than mine. Why? To this day I don't know the answer to that question. And at this point in my life, I've resigned myself to stop asking.

I do believe we live in a fallen world, where suffering and disease run rampant. It's surely our obligation to help the sick, pray for the sick, and relieve suffering whenever possible. But until we stand in eternity, pain will never completely come to an end. It's simply an aspect of life, a difficult part of the human condition.

For those who've suffered tragic loss through the death of a child, I can't imagine the hurt or the potential for bitterness and anger. I know many have been crushed by what appears to be silence from heaven. Our hearts cry out,

"Why are some healed and others are not?" It seems so unfair. To make matters worse, some have been cruelly blamed for the very tragedy that befell them. They've been told they've done something wrong to deserve their suffering or that their faith wasn't strong enough to overcome the adversity. Many fragile hearts have been wounded over such twisted doctrine.

In reality, suffering touches all of us, on different levels, and only God knows the sincerity of anyone's prayer. We're simply not the judge. At times, I've seen people who did not believe they would be healed, whereas others prayed in faith for them. I have seen those who believed with all their hearts that they would pass from this world into the next without being healed in body. Ultimately, though, I'm convinced that God hears each and every cry. I believe his compassion is infinite, but his purpose is often far beyond our understanding. In scripture, we're taught never to blame those who suffer calamity.

And as Jesus passed by, he saw a man which was blind from

his birth. And his disciples asked him, saying, Master, who did sin,

this man, or his parents, that he was born blind? Jesus answered,

Neither hath this man sinned, nor his parents: but that the works of

God should be made manifest in him. When he had thus spoken, he

spat on the ground, and made clay of the spittle, and he anointed the

eyes of the blind man with the clay. And said unto him, Go,

wash in the pool of Siloam. . . . He went his way therefore,

and washed, and came seeing.

JOHN 9:1–3 AND 6–7

For anyone whose heart breaks upon having his prayers denied, I understand. But most of all, God understands. Part of faith is trusting that God's ultimate decision is best, even if we can't see it in the natural or comprehend it with our heart. Many have wrestled with these questions simply to discover that aligning ourselves with God's plan is the only way to accept denied prayers. Perfection does not rest in the knowledge of God's order, but in submission to it. The order of God, the good pleasure of God, the will of God, the action of God, grace—all these are one and the same thing in this life.

Perfection is nothing else than the faithful cooperation of the soul with the work of God. This ultimate purpose of our life grows and increases in our souls secretly and without our knowledge.

JEAN-PIERRE DE CAUSSADE

We're admonished to discover God's will so our faith will align in prayer with his divine plan.

It is clear that he does not pray, who, far from uplifting himself to God, requires that God shall lower Himself to him, and who resorts to prayer not to stir the man in us to will what God wills, but only to persuade God to will what the man in us wills.

SAINT THOMAS AQUINAS

Some find it difficult to stir up their faith because they demand proof before they can trust. They function on the "I'll believe it when I see it" mentality. Yet all of us take much in faith on a daily basis. I don't know about you, but I can't see gravity (although I can see the effect of it). I can't see air (okay, sometimes I can—I live in California), but I still believe it's there. Certainly, I can't see and touch God, yet I can view the evidence of his presence. I overwhelmingly accept that so great a creation didn't happen without clear thought, planning, determination, and amazing love.

If you ask me how I believe in God, how God creates
Himself in me, and reveals Himself to me, my answer may
perhaps provoke your smiles or laughter, and even scandalize you.
I believe in God as I believe in my friends, because I feel the
breath of His affection, feel His invisible and intangible
hand drawing me, leading me, grasping me.

MIGUEL DE UNAMUNO

Often when we desire something, we can see it in our mind's eye. We believe it's good and ask for the blessing, although we can't comprehend how it will ever come to pass. Scripture shows us that it takes faith in the unknown to make it appear tangible.

> *Now faith is the substance of things hoped for,*
> *the evidence of things not seen.*

HEBREWS 11:1

As we spend time in prayer and act on the measure of faith we're all given, we'll come to better know the one we're seeking.

Through this relationship, a bond is formed, and our faith continues to grow. Faith is indeed the energy of our whole universe directed to the highest form of being. Faith gives stability to our view of the universe.

By faith we are convinced that our impressions of things without are not dreams or delusions, but, for us, true representations of our environment. By faith we are convinced that the signs of permanence, order, progress, which we observe in nature are true. By faith we are convinced that fellowship is possible with our fellow man and with God.

B. F. WESTCOTT

To embrace the virtue of faith, we must seek God diligently. Surely we live in a fast-paced, throw-it-out-there-quick-and-see-where-it-sticks culture.

Yet sincere seeking isn't accomplished in a moment. Most of us have hollered out fast prayers for help and thankfully had them abundantly answered. Having faith, however, requires us to consistently seek God's presence, plan, and purpose.

After all, scripture clearly teaches, it's not just the gift we seek but also the Giver himself.

But without faith it is impossible to please him: for he that cometh to God must believe that he is, and that he is a rewarder of them that diligently seek him.

———————

HEBREWS 11:6

In contrast with those who attempt to use faith as a tool for personal gain, there are others equally afraid to approach the Almighty with their problems at all.

They might reason, Who am I to ask the Master of the Universe to take note of my situation? Who am I to bother him with my insignificant problems?

Yet the very essence of our faith seems to cry out, He is more than desirous of a relationship with all of creation and has a heart toward meeting our needs.

There's a clear balance between those who are arrogant and those too insecure to ask for help at all. Reach out in faith. Because of love, scripture shows, you will be heard.

Humble yourselves therefore under the mighty hand
of God, that he may exalt you in due time: Casting all your care
upon him, for he careth for you.

———————

1 PETER 5:6–7

Yes, casting all our cares upon him—doesn't the mere thought sound inviting? With God so willing, why would you ever choose to carry your burdens alone? Give them over to the Creator, asking for faith to come alive in your being to restore you once more to a desired haven of rest.

Tips for Embracing
the Virtue of Faith

* Understand that everyone (including you) has been given a measure of faith.

* Don't keep your eyes on the problem; keep them on God, who has infinite abilities, answers, and solutions.

* Remember that faith even as small as a mustard seed can still move mountains. No problem is ever too big for God.

* Seek the Giver, not just the gift. For it's in our relationship with the Creator that our faith grows and our life takes on new meaning.

* Check the nature of your prayer—are you praying amiss?

* Desire God's will, not your own. As much as we think we know best, only our Creator knows the nuances in life that will achieve the ultimate good.

* Look at the bigger picture; faith is believing in what you can't see, even if it seems impossible.